# I Will Always Be Your Whore (Love Songs for Billy Corgan)

♥    ♥    ♥

## Alexandra Naughton

*Punk ♥ Hostage ♥ Press*

**I Will Always Be Your Whore**
**(Love Songs for Billy Corgan)**
Alexandra Naughton

©Punk Hostage Press 2014


ISBN-10: 1940213916

ISBN-13: 978-1-940213-91-0


Punk Hostage Press
P.O. Box 1869
Hollywood CA 90078

*www.punkhostagepress.com*


Introduction: Carrie Hunter

Cover Design:  Geoff Melville & Oliver Dillon

Cover Photo & Author Photo: Joe Carrow

Editor: A. Razor

Some of these poems have appeared
(in one form or another) in:
*Dusie, Gesture, Out of Our, Heartcloud, Guerrilla Graffiti
Magazine, Thousand
Shades of Gray,* and *voicemailpoems.org*

# Editor's Acknowledgments

This is a type of book I like to look for as a reader and as a publisher. A concise package with multiple abstractions that can blur lines between topic and genre, as well as tap into deep emotional states with a reflective voice. A journey into the soul of the writer inside of a vehicle that represents the cultural algorithm hammer that is constantly at work against our collective souls in this world.

And then there is the love aspect here, one that tangles it all up nicely from beginning to end, our greatest paramour of emotional achievement sliced up nicely with an obsessive-compulsive desire and served with a musicality so bold it provides a multi-media rock n' roll soundtrack experience that jumps off the page and mangles the senses.

Alexandra Naughton put out an effort here that Iris and I both found immediately intriguing and emotionally provocative. We are proud to present Alexandra's work here in this book that is a culmination of a great creative effort on her part and the support of a community of writers and artists that contributed to the final outcome of this presentation.

Firstly, we are honored to have such a brilliant introduction from Carrie Hunter as well as an equally glowing testimonial gracing the back cover from Amy Berkowitz. Their contributions bookend Alexandra's so well with well timed insight into the writer and her work presented here.

I would also like to gratefully acknowledge the work of Kimberly Kim in not only introducing me to Alexandra's work, but being a crucial element in providing support and feedback for all the work we do at Punk Hostage Press and Words As Works.

We want to show appreciation for the photographic work of Joe Carrow and the artistic design support of Geoff

Melville and Oliver Dillon to bring together the crucial elements of the author's photo and the book cover.

We hope this book strikes a nerve or several and finds a home in your heart where it will always be there for you.

- A. Razor, November 2013

# Introduction

There is an ironic, secretive sadness about Alexandra
Naughton's *I Will Always Be Your Whore.* I say ironic,
because these poems seem, in their nostalgia, slightly a
fantasy of sadness, something like a forecast of the burial
of a secret, of a hurt, and of the use of the hurt. These
poems seem to want to bruise each other while grasping
for another savior, not contained within the broken ideal
of Billy Corgan. They seem to want quite other than what
is being spoken of, within the wilting jailed flowering of
the poems' sentence.

Naughton's deadpan is a kinky kinetic matrix. A mix of
prose poems mixed with poetry lines mixed with prose.
Becoming other as act of becoming the self, or selves: "I
want to be your thoughts. I want to be your blood. I want
to be your capillaries. I want to be your tendons. Your spit.
Your zits. Your food. I want to be that flash of energy
when you conceive a phrase." Command as magic. The
urge toward destruction. Sediment. How layering functions
as desire, a desire to become sediment with one another.
Fear, nervousness, hurt, being afraid to look. Looking but
not reading. Knowing but not understanding. Emphatic
nostalgia. Wanting washing waiting, its own useless
diatribe against-againstness.

We see how the desire for attention comes from boredom.
How the incomplete coda turns into fermata. How the
poet surrounds herself with dislikes in order to make
something new happen. We see how the fermata of hurt is
repressed and becomes inertia. We see love that is not love
but a desire for love and then hurtling from love. We see a
one-sided sight, halved opening, halved light, halved
knowing. The book ends, half-fought, with a star in her
throat. Whether it is being swallowed, being born, or both
at once, it is regardless clearing the space for a new voice, a
new self, a new trajectory. We wait "stretched out like a
prostitute and just as calm."

- Carrie Hunter, *The Incompossible,* Black Radish Books

## Liner Notes/Dedication

I wrote these love song poems for Billy Corgan and a ghost.

Every poem has a corresponding song written by Billy Corgan. They are mostly Smashing Pumpkins songs, but there are a few Billy Corgan solo songs, as well as songs he wrote for other artists (like "Dying," which was recorded by Hole).

The poems can be read on their own, but you may wish to play the accompanying song while reading each piece.

I hope you enjoy them.

Dedication:

This book is dedicated to my team. I love you. Thanks for putting me on.

Alexandra Naughton   November 2013

**Playlist –**

love song # 1 ["Ava Adore"]

love song # 2 ["Love"]

love song # 3 ["X.Y.U."]

love song # 4 ["By Starlight"]

love song # 5 ["Do You Close Your Eyes"]

love song # 6 ["Soma"]

love song # 7 ["Czarina"]

love song #8 ["Luna"]

love song # 9 ["Suffer"]

love song #10 ["Lily (My One and Only)"]

love song # 11 ["Disarm"]

love song # 12 ["Thru The Eyes of Ruby"]

love song # 13 ["Thirty-Three"]

love song # 14 ["Astral Planes"]

love song # 15 ["Dying"]

love song # 16 ["Mayonnaise"]

love song # 17 ["Cherub Rock"]

love song # 18 ["Perfect"]

love song # 19 ["Blank Page"]

**Playlist [cont.] –**

love song # 20 ["Bodies"]

love song # 21 ["Crush"]

love song #22 ["Stand Inside Your Love"]

love song # 23 ["Ava Adore (Sadlands demo)"]

love song # 24 ["Set the Ray to Jerry"]

love song #25 ["Rhinoceros"]

love song #26 ["Tristessa"]

love song # 27 ["Try, Try, Try"]

love song #28 ["Feelium"]

love Song #29 ["Think You Know"]

we must never be apart we must never be apart we must never be apart we must never be apart we must never be ap art we must never be apart we must never be apart we must never be apart we must never be apart we must never be apart we must never be apart we must never be apart we must never be apart we must never be apart we must never be apart we must never be apart we must never be apart we must never be apart we must never be apart we must never be apart we must never be apart we must never be apart we must never be apart we must never be apart we must never be apart we must never be apart we must never be apart we must never be apart we must never be apart we must never be apart we must never be apart we must never be apart we must never be apart we must never be apart we must never be apart we must never be apart we must never be apart we must never be apart we must never be apart we must never be apart we must never be.

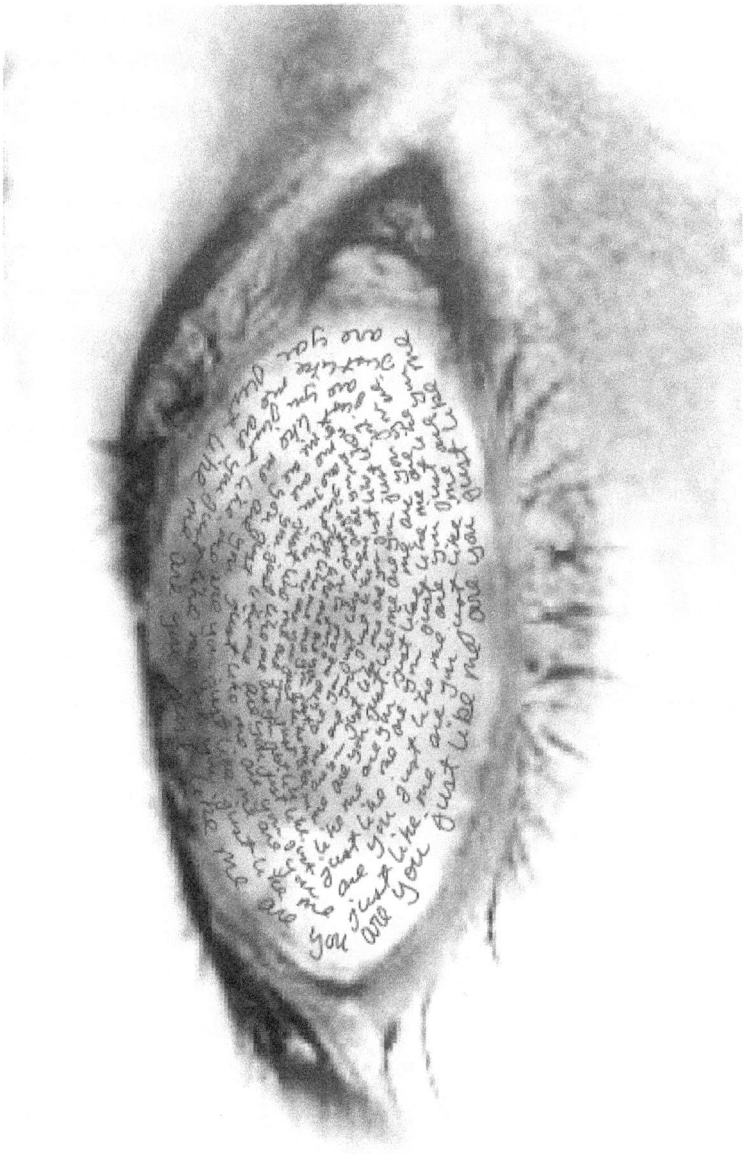

## love song # 1 ["Ava Adore"]

It's you that I adore.
I will always be your whore.

You will always be the object.
I will always be your object.

You will always be the subject.
I will always be your subject.

## love song # 2 ["Love"]

I read DH Lawrence on the train. I write sonnets on the toilet. I wear bras that make my breasts sit higher than they would without a bra. I used to worry that my breasts were too small but I don't anymore. I wonder if I am your muse. I think you are my muse. I stare into space and forget where I'm going. I untie my hair and tie it back up again.

I eat Vietnamese sandwiches with extra sriracha. I wear colorful tights with patterned dresses and make sriracha polka stains. I write poems in my head then write them down on receipts and bank statements. I write poems in my head and try to remember them when I don't have a pen; try to remember the poems in my head until I can find or borrow a pen. I listen to one album over and over again until I kill it dead. I drink tea with lemon and no honey. I drink black espresso and hot water and nothing else. I untie my hair and tie it back up again.

I write poems that I don't really want my family to read. I publish poems that my mom thinks are depressing. I publish poems about you that say things I can't say to you. I wonder what you think about, who you think about. I stare into space and wonder why I'm doing this. I smoke and I'm not sure if I'm inhaling correctly. I untie my hair and tie it back up again.

I think about painting my nails, but don't. I tape pictures on my wall that remind me of friends I don't see anymore. I buy groceries from the liquor store. I read Jean Rhys on a sunken mattress. I watch TV shows with predictable plot lines. I brush my teeth with a manual toothbrush even though I own an electric toothbrush. I laugh out loud on BART while reading Hunter S. Thompson, and then look around. I untie my hair and tie it back up again.

I miss you when you are not next to me. I think of ways to pass the time. I think about writing another letter to you. I have daydreams about us folding into each other like clay. I roll and chain smoke one spliff after another. I look in the mirror and dance to music that I liked in high-school. I try to remember how many times I've told the sycamore story. I untie my hair and tie it back up again.

## love song # 3 ["X.Y.U."]

I've got a problem but I'm not a stupid girl.

I know the deep shit I want to share with you.

This is how my garden grows. This is how I treat my ghosts.

This is where I make my home. This is where I leave my wound.

You know the secret I can't tell. You know the secrets I can keep.

You know where I bury my promises. And you know that I don't forget.

## love song # 4 ["By Starlight"]

You want to be my thoughts.

I want to be your thoughts, you say.

You are in my thoughts, I say. I mean. Not all of them, I think about other stuff too, but you're in there. My cheeks are hot and I touch the right one blood molding like autumn leaves.

And you say I want to be your thoughts.

I want to be your thoughts. I want to be your blood. I want to be your capillaries. I want to be your tendons. Your spit. Your zits. Your food. I want to be that flash of energy when you conceive a phrase.

I don't even know what to say.

## love song # 5 ["Do You Close Your Eyes"]

Turn clockwise in front of bathroom mirrors.
Chant soft gutturals, walking slow and careful.

Feel prongs against abdomen, sweat beading.
Spit while speaking. Spit your secrets on me.

Take everything as is and nothing more.
Be cautious of flattery and lashes.
And even more so with cut bottom lips.

Sell out. Overthink. Spend it all. Kill me.

You know I will pick blooms and walk with you.
You know I will cry when I think of you.
You know I will come when you want me to.
You know I will run away if things are real.
You know I have a place to keep your secret.

Do you make a wish when you kiss me?

# love song # 6 ["Soma"]

I want to smother each other in everything we see so much that it feels like nothing. I want to build walls around us together so that it's just us in this small sheetrock space sheltering each other, and we're intertwined, and we can feel every breath, and every whisper, so every movement makes me shake, and we can just look at each other and the drywall. I want to wrap ourselves in one another like we're one person and not even dusty daylight will come between us so we're sticking and stinking and we're parading around so people will be like "what the fuck was that?"

I want to envelop each other, like 47 guitar tracks layered one on top of one on top of one on top of one on top of one on top of one on top of one on top of one on top of one on top of one on top of one on top of one on top of one on top of one on top of one on top of one on top of one on top of one on top of one on top of one on top of one on top of one on top of one on top of one on top of one on top of one on top of one on top of one on top of one on top of one on top of one on top of one on top of one on top of one on top of one on top of one on top of one on top of one on top of one on top of one on top of one on top of one on top of one on top of one on top of one on top of one on top of one on top of one on top of one on top of one on top of one on top of one on top of one on top of one so we are just crumbled paper bags and comic books stacked on the floor.

# love song # 7 ["Czarina"]

I am staring at the wood grain of this table and you're sitting right next to me. I wonder what you're thinking. I wonder if you feel like you're regretting coming here or if you're just afraid to say the wrong thing. I wonder if you're wondering the same about me. Um.

We drink tea and I watch as you read the leaves. Eyes pick intermittently. I'm scared to really say anything. Oooh, hot. Scared to really look. We see from the corners.

I spill my mug.

We small laugh, talk about bad horror movies, our favorite scenes and favorite monsters, how we watch too much TV, about too-savvy ex-government agents and Law & Order, then I propose we go home and watch 1990-1994-- you know, the good years.

Outside in the moonlight it's cold but the silence warms us, soft and buzzing around us. I want to adorn your brow with scarlet blush, submit myself, let you braid my dreams.

I untie my hair and tie it back up again.

## love song #8 ["Luna"]

I dream of the same places, walking up hills, up cliff sides, wobbling, holding a paper cup and looking straight ahead, along shorelines and on boardwalks and I know you're there with me but I can't see you.

### love song # 9 ["Suffer"]

Will I hurt?
Yes I will.
Will I hurt?
Yes I will.
Will I hurt?
Yes I will.
Will I hurt?
Yes I will.
Will I hurt?
Yes I will.
Will I hurt?
Yes I will.
Will I hurt?
Yes I will.
Will I hurt?
Yes I will.
Will I hurt?
Yes I will.
Will I hurt?
Yes I will.
Will I hurt?
Yes I will.
Will I hurt?
Yes I will.
Will I hurt?
Yes I will.
Will I hurt?

Yes I will.

I will hurt for you.

## love song #10 ["Lily (My One and Only)"]

Numb lips kiss but can't hold a cigarette.

Looking at words on the screen, not reading, anticipating something.

Not wanting to be popular, not trying to explain yourself.

Do you know who is wearing your blue bathrobe.

## love song # 11 ["Disarm"]

I keep receipts that remind me of you stuffed in my wallet.

## love song # 12 ["Thru The Eyes of Ruby"]

Be emphatic. Seduce in non sequiturs and lace
sensors.

Romance as I sit owl-like on your fraying vintage sofa
bleeding words together and pacing.

Smear odes on shopping lists. Spew sonnets at
karaoke bars.

Make it so I can't tell if you're kidding or sincere.
Curse on my stubbed toes.

Lecture all the time. I am your student. Tell me how
innocence is tragic, but naiveté-- gullibility never
ending-- is death.

Kneel on raw rice grains. Propose that we do nothing.

## love song # 13 ["Thirty-Three"]

Do you know I am in your kitchen, washing.
Billy, do you know I am here waiting.
Do you know how long I have been.
Do you know why.
Do you see me combine soap and chicken grease.
Do you know my bruises, soft blue tender.
Do you hear my murmuring, get drunker caring less.
Do you get my reasons or my gestures.
Do you feel my stomach ache.

I know where you keep the tea and biscuits.
I know the pointless early evenings.
I see the beauty in your marked up words.
I see how stupid I can be.
I just want to turn you on. I just want to turn you on.

## love song # 14 ["Astral Planes"]

We are in bed together. I am on the window side. You are on the weird side. Your floor is dusty and papers are all over the place, like a window is open except my side has the window and my side is neat.

We are in bed and you are on your laptop. You are almost always on your laptop. You are using your laptop to look at tour updates. I am lying next to you and staring at the dust webs on the ceiling on your side of the room.

You are on your laptop and in the dark room the blue light from the screen bounces on my face and makes me squint to look at the ceiling webs. I touch your arm and you are now looking at photos from the last show and I get out from under the covers and decide I am your cat.

I scratch my face on your laptop screen and crawl around in a circle to make myself comfortable, nudging the screen. I crawl around in a circle, and crawl around in a circle, and crawl around in a circle until I feel comfortable and plop my chin onto your forearm. You look up from your laptop screen.

You pat my head and I purr. You pat my butt and I purr. I am your cat. I am your laptop.

## love song # 15 ["Dying"]

I don't have feelings. I'm in love with you and I'm writing poems. I don't have feelings and I'm writing poems for you and getting sicker as I go on. I'm writing poems for you because I don't have feelings. I'm in love with you and writing poems is the only way I can stop breathing weird.

I don't have feelings. I'm in love with you and I'm writing poems for you. I write these poems and put your name on them because I feel like you should probably know how much I think about you but I can't even say it to you directly. I mean, I say all the time, but not directly, like everything I do, and showing you these poems is kind of a cop out but I feel like that is how I have to do it. Maybe call in sick tomorrow.

I don't have feelings. I'm in love with you and I'm writing poems for you and feeling sadder because I don't think I'm worth the time.

## love song # 16 ["Mayonnaise"]

Infinite suck, like when I get cerebral with you.
Jaw tires and you hold my hand.

## love song # 17 ["Cherub Rock"]

Tell me all of your secrets.
And burn your nose in my chest.

Tell me all of your secrets.
Billy, let me get that eyelash.

Tell me all of your secrets.
Ask me to arch my back a little.

Tell me all of your secrets.
We talk about stir fry vegetables.

Tell me all of your secrets.
You fall asleep with the oven still on.

Tell me all of your secrets.
You say we are safe when we work.

Woe, cry
woe, cry.

Tell you all of my secrets.
Looking at the wall and breathing.

Tell you all of my secrets.
Feel my muscle move strange.

Tell you all of my secrets.
Every drop I bleed is yours.


Tell you all of my secrets.
This spot needs tending to.

Tell you all of my secrets.
So many things I poison myself.

Tell you all of my secrets.
Swallow me until I stop shaking.

Woe, cry
woe, cry.

## love song # 18 ["Perfect"]

I don't know if I can do this or if you even want to. Do you see me sitting here.

I'm a sponge, sopping, longing. Perched on this vinyl kitchen chair watching you butter toast. Watching dry crumbs flutter.

We slept in every room, the hallways and stairwells.

We took midnight walks through cemeteries midnight walks to all night diners midnight walks are our confessionals.

You showed me your collections of fuck ups. You showed me where it hurts.

I showed you where I made my marks. I show you how I grind my teeth.

I untie my hair and tie it back up again and you just stare.

## love song # 19 ["Blank Page"]

Letting a coda go and flourish, then stopping suddenly. Not even tapering. How can you be everything and nothing.

## love song # 20 ["Bodies"]

I'm wearing this perfume because I don't like it and it's reminding me that I need to fix my life.

## love song # 21 ["Crush"]

I'm surrounded by these people who I care about very
much yet they continue to keep failing me. And I feel
like everyone is like, you're not worth going home and
working on the poem. And I just want to feel safe.
And I just want to feel like what I'm doing is working.
And I wonder if it matters anyway. And I just want
you to hold me when I see you, drain the bad humor
a little. And press me down until I pass out.

## love song #22 ["Stand Inside Your Love"]

Like loving someone who is a ghost. Like loving someone who is not real is like loving someone you don't know, like loving someone who is a ghost. Like you can't see them but sometimes you can sense them and you wonder if maybe they sense you too. Like loving someone who is not reachable, not too far for phone calls, the physical space is not a factor, but you feel far away from even yourself when you think about them. Like you know them mostly in your head. Like standing alone in front of a mirror and seeing someone's hand on your shoulder. Like loving a ghost and wondering if they like this song, too. Like loving someone you can see but never touch. Like loving someone you can chase but never catch.

## love song # 23 ["Ava Adore (Sadlands demo)"]

In you I stub toes.
In you I chase flies.

In you I scream murder.
In you I taste lies.

In you I feel so petty.
In you I fake cries.

We must never be apart.

## love song # 24 ["Set the Ray to Jerry"]

Getting rich and finding fame won't change the mealy feeling inside.

We all want the same things, someone to walk with us to the store.

## love song #25 ["Rhinoceros"]

I'm the towel you use and don't wash for weeks.
I'm the spit cum crust on your roommate's sheets.

I'm your whore, your whore, your whore, your whore,
yours.
Your whore, your whore, your whore, your whore,
your whore.

I'm the stain on the BART train floor.
The hair in the drain, on the shower door.

I'm your whore, your whore, your whore, your whore,
yours.
Your whore, your whore, your whore, your whore,
your whore.

Your whore, your whore, your whore, and nothing
more.
Your whore, your little whore, your filthy whore.

Open your eyes, watch the light turn yellow.
Open your eyes, you don't see but I know.

## love song #26 ["Tristessa"]

Take me down to the trees. Make this gown green.
I am your dirty puzzle. I am yours to ponder over,
lose.

Porcelain and translucent and waiting.
Soft and cold like the moon and just as far.

My desk is messy with letters to you.
Everything I see I want to tell you.

You will wait. I will wait. You will wait and
I will wait. You will wait and I will wait.

Surely this will do. Surely this will do.

## love song # 27 ["Try, Try, Try"]

Stretched out like a prostitute and just as calm. Inside I am worms and shells, ashes and snot and something festering. I want to flee. Or at least think about getting up.

## love song #28 ["Feelium"]

Always not always sometimes but always sometimes never. Sometimes but sometimes never sometimes always sometimes not always. Never always. Never not always but sometimes always.

## love Song #29 ["Think You Know"]

you make me

      feel like a piece

      of star

   is glowing

   in my throat

*I keep receipts that remind me*

```
              7-ELEVEN
           14501 SAN PABLO AVE
        SAN PABLO CA 948062445
              5102368860
             STORE#: 24643
          THANKS FOR SHOPPING
             AT 7-ELEVEN

1 olypso 3 melon               2.49
1 CRV                          0.05
1 Snpple DazeLmnde16z          1.39F
1 CRV                          0.05F
2 SS Cgrlo Impls .89           1.78T
1 ZigZagFrnchOrng1.25          2.19T
1 Nwprt8xKg                    6.18T

TOTAL CRV                      0.10
SUBTOTAL                      14.13
SALES TAX ON 10.15             0.91
TOTAL DUE                     15.04
DEBIT                        15.04
ACCT#: xxxxxxxxxxxx8176
ACCT TYPE: DDA
APPROVAL#: 162543        AUTH CODE: 0
APPROVAL TIME: 182449
Maestro
STORE#: 24643
TERM# :00072464322 08
TERM SEQ#: 989362
REF# : 95000 85 005 0
APPROVED
```

*of you*   *stuffed in my wallet*

```
      CUSTOMER AGREES TO PAY THE ABOVE
     TOTAL AMOUNT  ACCORDING TO THE CARD
             HOLDERS AGREEMENT


             OH THANK HEAVEN
              FOR 7-ELEVEN
  T#01 0P01 TRN0827 09/03/2013 06:24 pm
```

*Photo by Joe Carrow*

Alexandra Naughton is a writer in Oakland, California. She
hopes Billy Corgan reads this book someday.

*Forthcoming from Punk Hostage Press –*

'When I Was A Dynamiter' *(2013)*
by Lee Quarnstrom

'Dead Lions' *(2013) by A.D. Winans*

'Where The Road Leads You' *(2013) by Diana Rose*

'Disgraceland' *(2014)*
by Iris Berry & Pleasant Gehamn

'Long Winded Tales of a Low Plains Drifter' *(2014)*
by A. Razor

'On The Boulevard Spoken Dreams' *(2014)*
by Iris Berry

'Dangerous Intersections' *(2014) by Annette Cruz*

'Driving All of the Horses at Once' *(2014)*
by Richard Modiano

'The Red Hook Giraffe' *(2014)*
by James Anthony Tropeano III

'Dreams Gone Mad with Hope' *(2014)*
by S.A. Griffin

'In The Shadow of the Hollywood Sign' *(2014)*
by Iris Berry

'Puro Purismo' *(2014) by A. Razor*